Please visit our website, www.garethstevens.com. For a free color catalog of all our high-quality books, call toll free 1-800-542-2595 or fax 1-877-542-2596.

Cataloging-in-Publication Data

Names: Banks, Rosie.
Title: Nasty swans / Rosie Banks.
Description: New York : Gareth Stevens Publishing, 2018. | Series: Cutest animals...that could kill you! | Includes index.
Identifiers: ISBN 9781538212714 (pbk.) | ISBN 9781538210895 (library bound) | ISBN 9781538210888 (6 pack)
Subjects: LCSH: Swans–Juvenile literature.
Classification: LCC QL696.A52 B36 2018 | DDC 598.4'18–dc23

First Edition

Published in 2018 by
Gareth Stevens Publishing
111 East 14th Street, Suite 349
New York, NY 10003

Designer: Sarah Liddell
Editor: Therese Shea

Photo credits: Cover, p. 1 Ihi/Shutterstock.com; wood texture used throughout Imageman/Shutterstock.com; slash texture used throughout d1sk/Shutterstock.com; pp. 4–5 Dima Zel/Shutterstock.com; p. 7 (mute swan) Dawn J Benko/Shutterstock.com; p. 7 (trumpeter swan) ArchonCodex/Shutterstock.com; p. 9 (main) Inc/Shutterstock.com; pp. 8–9 (black-necked swan) Christopher Elwell/Shutterstock.com; p. 11 TwilightArtPictures/Shutterstock.com; p. 13 Zocchi Roberto/Shutterstock.com; p. 15 Karel Gallas/Shutterstock.com; p. 17 Mikhailo/Shutterstock.com; p. 19 WoodysPhotos/Shutterstock.com; pp. 20–21 Zoran Matic/Shutterstock.com.

Printed in China

CPSIA compliance information: Batch #CW18GS: For further information contact Gareth Stevens, New York, New York at 1-800-542-2595.

CONTENTS

Words in the glossary appear in **bold** type the first time they are used in the text.

ANGRY BIRD

A swan glides across a lake. It swims silently. Water moves in gentle waves from its body. You may have seen swans swimming like this in a pond or lake. If you have, you may be surprised to learn that swans aren't always peaceful. They can be very unpleasant!

In fact, when swans are angry, they can be dangerous—even to people. Read on to find out how mad these birds can get and why it's always smart to keep them at a **distance**.

SWANS ARE **SYMBOLS** OF GRACE AND BEAUTY. DO YOU THINK THEY'RE CUTE? JUST DON'T GET TOO CLOSE!

BIG BIRDS

Swans are large birds that live on or near water, such as lakes, **marshes**, and other wetlands. They have a long neck, a heavy body, and big feet.

The largest swan **species** is the trumpeter swan. It can be more than 5 feet (1.5 m) long. Its **wingspan** can be 8 feet (2.4 m) from tip to tip. The mute swan is a bit smaller, but just as heavy. Both species can weigh 30 pounds (14 kg). They're some of the heaviest flying birds in the world!

THE DANGEROUS DETAILS

The trumpeter swan is named for its low call. Mute swans are usually mute, or make no sound. Both birds make sounds when they're angry, though!

MOST SWAN SPECIES ARE ALL WHITE WITH BLACK LEGS. THE TRUMPETER SWAN HAS A BLACK BILL. THE MUTE SWAN HAS AN ORANGE BILL WITH A BLACK SPOT ON THE TIP.

MUTE SWAN

TRUMPETER SWAN

WHERE IN THE WORLD?

Five swan species live in North America, the northern parts of Europe, and Asia. They include the trumpeter swan, mute swan, whooper swan, Bewick's swan, and whistling swan. All five are white. The black swan lives in Australia. Two species found in South America are the black-necked swan and the coscoroba swan.

Most species migrate, or fly long distances, to spend different seasons in different areas. They find their food in and around water, so they migrate before water freezes for the winter.

BLACK-NECKED SWAN

8

SWANS FLY WITH THEIR LONG NECK STICKING OUT. THEY FLAP THEIR WINGS SLOWLY.

THE DANGEROUS DETAILS

Black-necked swans of South America are very nasty! They're easy to spot because of the red growth on their bill.

9

LIFE IN THE WATER

Swans mostly eat plants and **algae**. They use their long neck to reach food underwater such as seaweed and grasses. When they wander onto land, they eat plants, seeds, and berries. They also eat bugs, fish eggs, and sometimes small fish.

Swans' **webbed** feet help power them through water. They also have a **gland** that produces oil that covers their feathers. The oil makes their feathers waterproof so they don't get cold. A layer of soft feathers near their skin, called down, keeps them warm, too.

STARTING A SWAN FAMILY

Swans aren't always on the water, but they stay close to it. They build large nests on land out of small branches and leaves.

After a male and female swan **mate**, the female lays between three and nine eggs in the nest. The female lays one egg every 12 to 24 hours. Then, the mother swan sits on the eggs to keep them warm until they **hatch**. This is called incubation. The eggs hatch about 4 to 6 weeks later.

THE DANGEROUS DETAILS

The father swan stays near the nest to keep the eggs safe. He may sit on the eggs if something happens to the mother.

SWANS EAT A LOT BEFORE THEY SIT ON THEIR EGGS. THEY DON'T WANT TO LEAVE THE NEST LONG WHILE THE EGGS ARE INCUBATING.

SWEET CYGNETS

Baby swans are called cygnets (SIHG-nuhtz). They're born with their eyes open and covered in down. They start swimming just a few days later. Cygnets begin to fly when they're around 4 months old.

Cygnets have a lot of enemies in nature since they're not big enough to **protect** themselves yet. Predators include crows, **herons**, turtles, foxes, and large fish. Both mother and father swans live with their cygnets for up to 9 months to protect them.

THE DANGEROUS DETAILS

Swans may flap their wings and make a hissing sound to warn creatures to stay away from their nest!

CYGNETS BY THE NUMBERS

1 DAY OLD: LEAVE THE NEST

2 DAYS OLD: LEARN TO SWIM

2 WEEKS OLD: FEED THEMSELVES

10 WEEKS OLD: HAVE FULL FEATHERS

17 WEEKS OLD: LEARN TO FLY

9 MONTHS OLD: LEAVE THEIR PARENTS

2 YEARS OLD: FIND A MATE

IT TAKES MANY MONTHS BEFORE CYGNETS GROW THEIR ADULT FEATHERS.

15

PREDATORS AND PEOPLE

Adult swans don't have to fear many predators in the wild because they're so large. However, wolves, raccoons, and foxes hunt swans. And swans have another enemy: people!

People hunt swans for meat and for feathers. However, there are rules in some places about which species and how many swans can be killed on a hunt. These laws keep certain swan populations from getting too low. In some places, some swan populations are too large, so more hunting is allowed.

THE DANGEROUS DETAILS
Swans may attack each other. They don't like other swans in their territory.

MANY HUNTERS SHOOT WATERFOWL, OR BIRDS THAT LIVE ON OR IN WATER. THEY MAY USE DOGS TO RETRIEVE, OR BRING BACK, THE BIRDS THEY HUNT.

17

A DEADLY ATTACK

Swans are deadly serious about taking care of their cygnets. They'll even leave the nest to attack animals—and people—that they think are dangerous to them.

In 2012, two swans attacked a man's boat. The boat overturned, and the man tried to swim to shore. But the birds attacked the man, and he drowned. Likely, the swans had a nest nearby. Rare attacks like this are reminders to stay away from swans and their nests when possible.

THE DANGEROUS DETAILS

Swans may peck and pinch with their bill. Ouch!

SWANS OFTEN USE THEIR WINGS AS **WEAPONS.** THE WINGS CAN HURT IF THEY HIT YOU AT TOP SPEED!

STAY AWAY, SWANS!

Remember, swans are just trying to protect their families. Many wild animals do this. Swans that are nasty while protecting their eggs and cygnets are often quite peaceful for the rest of the year. However, you can never tell how they're going to act toward you. That's why you should always stay away from swans and all wild animals.

Swans are beautiful animals to watch from a distance. Enjoy their beauty from far away!

SWANS KEEP THEIR TERRITORIES HEALTHY BY EATING PLANTS THAT CAN OVERGROW AND BY SPREADING SEEDS TO GROW NEW PLANTS.

GLOSSARY

algae: plantlike living things that are mostly found in water

distance: a point or place that is far away from another point or place. Also, the amount of space between two places or things.

gland: a body part that makes something the body uses

hatch: to break open so young can come out

heron: a large bird that has long legs and a long neck and bill

marsh: an area of soft, wet land that has many grasses and other plants

mate: to come together to make babies

protect: to guard from harm

species: a group of animals that are alike and can produce young animals

symbol: an object that stands for an idea or quality

weapon: something used for fighting, attacking, or defending

webbed: having pieces of skin that connect all the toes on a foot

wingspan: the distance from the tip of one wing of a bird to the tip of the other wing

FOR MORE INFORMATION

BOOKS

Bodden, Valerie. *Swans*. Mankato, MN: Creative Education, 2009.

Gray, Leon. *Trumpeter Swan: The World's Largest Waterbird.* New York, NY: Bearport Publishing, 2013.

Horak, Steven A. *Swans and Other Swimming Birds*. Chicago, IL: World Book, 2012.

WEBSITES

Swan Facts for Kids
www.coolkidfacts.com/swan-facts-for-kids/
Read more about these sometimes angry birds.

Swans
www.dkfindout.com/us/animals-and-nature/birds/swans/
Hear what a mute swan sounds like when it does make noise!

Publisher's note to educators and parents: Our editors have carefully reviewed these websites to ensure that they are suitable for students. Many websites change frequently, however, and we cannot guarantee that a site's future contents will continue to meet our high standards of quality and educational value. Be advised that students should be closely supervised whenever they access the Internet.

INDEX